HOW TO USE RECESSION TO BECOME RICH

COMMON MAN GUIDE

MYSTIC GURU

Made with ❤ on the Notion Press Platform
www.notionpress.com

Dear readers,

This book, "How to Use Recession to Become Rich," is dedicated to the common man. To the person who may not have a background in finance or economics, but who is determined to improve their financial situation. To the person who has been impacted by a recession, but who refuses to give up on their dreams of wealth and prosperity.

In recent years, recessions have become an all-too-familiar reality. As economies around the world have suffered, many have lost their jobs, their homes, and their savings. Yet despite the challenges and hardships, there is a glimmer of hope. There are those who have used recessions to their advantage, turning financial adversity into a pathway to wealth.

This book is for those who believe that wealth is not just for the lucky few, but for anyone with the courage, determination, and knowledge to pursue it. Whether you are just starting out on your financial journey or you have experienced a setback, this book is designed to give you the tools and strategies you need to build wealth, even in the most challenging of economic conditions.

The truth is that recessions are not simply a time of hardship, but also a time of opportunity. Those who are prepared and equipped with the right knowledge can use recessions to find deals, invest in undervalued assets, and secure financial security for themselves and their families.

It is our hope that this book will empower you to take control of your finances, to see the opportunities in recessions, and to build the wealth and security that you deserve. Whether you are a young person just starting out in life, or a seasoned professional looking to protect and grow your wealth, this book is for you.

We believe that anyone can become rich, regardless of their background or circumstances. All it takes is a commitment to learning, a willingness to take risks, and the determination to succeed. So let us begin this journey together, as we explore the secrets of using recessions to become rich.

Contents

Contents

Foreword

Foreword

The idea of becoming rich during a recession might seem counterintuitive to many, but with the right knowledge and approach, it can indeed be possible. The current economic landscape presents unique challenges and opportunities, and this book, "How to Use Recession to Become Rich," aims to equip the common man with the tools and strategies needed to navigate these times and come out ahead.

Recessions can be daunting and stressful for most people. They bring about job loss, financial insecurity, and uncertainty about the future. However, as the old adage goes, every challenge presents an opportunity. In this case, the opportunity is to build wealth during a recession. This book is a guide for the average person who wants to turn the economic downturn into a financial upswing.

The book covers a range of topics that are crucial for financial success during a recession. From understanding the economics of recessions, to identifying opportunities in a downturn, to building a recession-proof portfolio, the authors provide practical and actionable advice. The book also delves into the psychology of wealth building during a recession, highlighting the importance of a strong support network, disciplined focus, and continuous education.

The authors share their insights and experiences, providing real-life examples of how to make smart and informed financial decisions during a recession. They cover a range of investment strategies, from stock market investments to real estate, as well as alternative sources of income and passive income streams. The book also touches on the importance of reducing expenses and maximizing savings, as well as how to navigate unemployment and job loss.

One of the key takeaways from this book is the importance of being prepared for the next recession. The authors emphasize the need to continually educate oneself financially and to build a strong, diverse portfolio. They also discuss the importance of making informed and strategic investments and being financially agile in changing times.

Another important aspect of the book is its emphasis on entrepreneurship. The authors share their insights on how to build a recession-resilient business and the opportunities that can arise during a downturn. They also provide tips on leveraging technology to increase income and finding government assistance programs that can help during tough times.

In conclusion, this book is a comprehensive guide for anyone looking to make the most of a recession and build wealth. Whether you are an experienced investor or just starting out, the authors provide practical and actionable advice that can help you navigate these challenging times and come out ahead. The book is written in an easy-to-understand and engaging style, making it accessible to anyone looking to build a better financial future. So, whether you are a student, a working professional, or a retiree, this book is for you.

In these uncertain times, the knowledge and strategies outlined in this book can serve as a roadmap for financial success. So, pick up a copy today and start your journey towards financial freedom and stability.

Introduction

Recession is often seen as a time of economic uncertainty, job loss, and financial instability. However, it can also be an opportunity for those who are prepared and know how to use it to their advantage. In this book, "How to Use Recession to Become Rich," we will explore strategies and techniques for turning economic hardship into financial prosperity. Whether you're a seasoned investor or a newcomer to personal finance, you'll find valuable insights and practical advice for making the most of a recession. Our goal is to empower you with the knowledge and skills needed to turn a potentially negative situation into a positive one.

The book is written in an easy-to-understand language and is suitable for people from all walks of life, regardless of their financial background or education. The chapters are designed to provide a comprehensive understanding of how to use a recession to your advantage, covering topics like real estate investing, stock market strategies, alternative sources of income, and financial education. By following the tips and guidance provided in this book, you can take control of your financial future, even in challenging times. So, if you're ready to turn a recession into an opportunity for wealth building, let's get started!

Note : "The book is written in essay format, with each chapter covering a unique topic. Not every chapter is meant for everyone. For example, some may excel in real estate, others in cryptocurrency, and others in the money market. It's best to build skills in areas where you already have expertise. The book is designed in a way that allows you to read individual chapters and still receive the message.

If you choose to read the entire book, you may find some information repeated, as each chapter is written as a standalone essay for individuals with varying skill sets. If you have expertise in a particular field, focus on those chapters for optimal results."

CHAPTER ONE

Understanding the economics of recessions

Economic recessions are a natural part of the business cycle and can have a significant impact on individuals, businesses, and the overall economy. While the topic of economics can be complex and confusing, it is essential for everyone to have a basic understanding of how recessions work and what they can mean for our personal finances. This essay will provide a straightforward explanation of the economics of recessions for the common man.

A recession is typically defined as a period of economic contraction that lasts for at least two consecutive quarters. During this time, the gross domestic product (GDP), which is a measure of the total value of goods and services produced in an economy, decreases. Additionally, employment and consumer spending also tend to decline during a recession. These factors can lead to a downward spiral of economic activity, which can be difficult to reverse without intervention.

The causes of a recession are often complex and multifaceted. Some of the most common factors include a decline in consumer confidence, a reduction in business investment, and an increase in the cost of borrowing. For example, if consumers are feeling uncertain about the future, they may be less likely to make big purchases, like buying a new car or a house. This reduction in consumer spending can have a ripple effect on the economy, causing businesses to reduce their own spending and investments.

At the same time, an increase in the cost of borrowing, such as an increase in interest rates, can make it more expensive for businesses to borrow money to invest in new projects. This can also contribute to a decline in economic activity. Furthermore, factors such as natural disasters, political instability, and global economic conditions can also play a role in causing a recession.

While a recession can be difficult for everyone, it can be especially challenging for those who have limited financial resources. For example, individuals who have lost their jobs or are facing wage cuts may struggle to pay their bills and meet their basic needs. Additionally, a decrease in consumer spending can lead to businesses closing their doors, which can further reduce employment opportunities.

Despite these challenges, there are ways for individuals to prepare for and potentially benefit from a recession. For example, building an emergency fund and reducing debt can help individuals weather an economic downturn. Additionally, individuals can also seek out alternative sources of income, such as starting a side business or freelance work.

Investing can also be a good way to potentially benefit from a recession. For example, during a recession, stock prices may be lower than usual, providing an opportunity for investors to buy quality stocks at a discount. However, it is important to understand that investing can also be risky, and individuals should only invest money that they can afford to lose.

In conclusion, understanding the economics of recessions is important for everyone, as they can have a significant impact on our personal finances. While a recession can be challenging, there are steps individuals can take to prepare for and potentially benefit from an economic downturn. Building an emergency fund, reducing debt, seeking alternative sources of income, and making informed investment decisions can all help individuals weather a recession and potentially come out ahead in the long run.

CHAPTER TWO

Identifying opportunities in a downturn

Recessions can be a difficult and challenging time for everyone, including the common man. The economy slows down, businesses struggle, and people lose their jobs. However, recessions also provide unique opportunities for those who know how to identify and capitalize on them. In this essay, we will discuss the various ways in which the common man can identify and take advantage of opportunities during a downturn.

One of the most significant opportunities during a recession is the ability to purchase assets at a discount. When the economy is in a downturn, the prices of stocks, real estate, and other assets typically drop, making them more affordable for the average person. For example, if you've always wanted to invest in real estate, a recession can be an excellent time to buy a property. Not only will you be able to purchase it at a lower price, but you'll also have the chance to hold onto the property until the market recovers and its value increases.

Another opportunity that arises during a recession is the ability to start a business. With many people losing their jobs, the demand for new businesses and services increases. This is a great time for the common man to start a small business, offering a new product or service that fills a gap in the market. With careful planning, hard work, and a little bit of luck, this could lead to a successful and profitable business that will provide a source of income for years to come.

Moreover, the common man can also take advantage of a recession by improving their education and skills. With many people losing their jobs, it's an excellent time to upgrade your education and skills. This could mean taking courses in areas that interest you, or learning a new skill that is in high demand. For example, during the current pandemic, many people have turned to online learning and taken courses in areas such as computer programming, graphic design, or web development. Improving your education and skills can lead to better job opportunities and a higher salary when the economy recovers.

Additionally, recessions can also provide an opportunity for the common man to pay off debt. With the economy slowing down and many people losing their jobs, it's an excellent time to focus on reducing expenses and paying off debt. This can include credit card debt, car loans, or student loans. By reducing debt, you'll not only be improving your financial situation, but you'll also be reducing the stress and anxiety that come with owing money.

Lastly, it's crucial for the common man to stay informed about the economy and the markets. This can involve reading financial news and websites, listening to podcasts, or attending seminars. By staying informed, you'll be able to better understand the current economic climate and identify opportunities that arise during a recession.

In conclusion, while recessions can be a challenging time for the common man, they also provide unique opportunities. These opportunities include the ability to purchase assets at a discount, start a business, improve your education and skills, pay off debt, and stay informed about the economy and the markets. By taking advantage of these opportunities, the common man can improve their financial situation, reduce stress and anxiety, and lay the foundation for a more secure future.

CHAPTER THREE

Building a recession-proof portfolio

Building a recession-proof portfolio during a recession is a smart financial strategy that can help protect and grow your wealth. A recession-proof portfolio is designed to withstand market downturns and provide stability in uncertain times. As a common man, it can be challenging to navigate the financial landscape during a recession, but with the right strategies and tools, it is possible to build a portfolio that can weather the storm.

First and foremost, it is important to understand the economics of a recession. A recession is a period of economic decline characterized by declining Gross Domestic Product (GDP), high unemployment, and reduced consumer spending. During a recession, the stock market often experiences significant losses, and many businesses struggle to survive.

The key to building a recession-proof portfolio is to diversify your investments. Diversification means spreading your investment dollars across different types of assets, such as stocks, bonds, real estate, and commodities. This helps to reduce the risk of losing money in a single market or sector.

One strategy to consider is to allocate a portion of your portfolio to bonds. Bonds are debt instruments that provide a fixed income stream and are generally considered to be less risky than stocks. During a recession, the value of bonds may rise as investors flock to the safety of fixed-income investments.

Another strategy is to invest in real estate. Real estate can provide a source of income through rental properties and can also offer long-term growth potential. However, it is important to understand the local real estate market and to invest in properties that are likely to retain or increase in value over time.

Another way to reduce risk is to invest in low-cost index funds. Index funds are passively managed funds that track the performance of a specific market index, such as the S&P 500. Index funds offer a low-cost and simple way to diversify your portfolio and gain exposure to a broad range of stocks.

It is also important to have a long-term perspective when building a recession-proof portfolio. The stock market is volatile in the short term, but over the long term, it has historically produced strong returns. By investing in a diversified portfolio and holding onto your investments for the long term, you can weather the ups and downs of the market and benefit from its long-term growth potential.

Along with investing in the stock market, it is also important to focus on reducing expenses and maximizing savings. During a recession, it may be tempting to cut back on savings or to spend more in an effort to boost the economy. However, this can be a dangerous strategy, as it can lead to a reduction in wealth over time. Instead, focus on reducing unnecessary expenses, such as dining out or entertainment, and consider increasing your savings rate to build a strong financial foundation.

Entrepreneurship is also a strategy to consider during a recession. Starting a small business can provide a source of income and can also offer the potential for significant growth. However, it is important to carefully evaluate the market and to choose a business that is likely to succeed in a recessionary environment.

In conclusion, building a recession-proof portfolio during a recession is a smart financial strategy that can help protect and grow your wealth. By diversifying your investments, focusing on reducing expenses and maximizing savings, and having a long-term perspective, you can build a portfolio that can weather market downturns and provide stability in uncertain times. Remember to continually educate yourself about personal finance, the stock market, and the economy, and to seek professional advice if necessary.

CHAPTER FOUR

Real estate investments during a recession

Real Estate Investments During Recession

Recession is a difficult economic phase characterized by a decrease in gross domestic product (GDP), higher unemployment, and reduced consumer spending. Despite the adverse conditions, there are still opportunities for investing and growing wealth, particularly in real estate. For a common man, real estate investments during a recession can be a smart move if approached correctly. In this essay, we will discuss why real estate can be a good investment during a recession and how to make informed decisions for maximum returns.

Why Invest in Real Estate During a Recession?

During a recession, the demand for housing decreases, which leads to a drop in property prices. While this may seem like a negative, it is an opportunity for investors to purchase properties at lower prices. When the economy bounces back, property prices tend to increase, resulting in potentially significant returns on investment.

Additionally, rental demand remains steady during a recession as people opt to rent rather than buy. This provides an opportunity for real estate investors to generate passive income through rental properties. Furthermore, the reduced competition in the real estate market during a recession means that there are fewer bidders for properties, making it easier for investors to negotiate favorable terms and purchase properties at lower prices.

Factors to Consider When Investing in Real Estate During a Recession

Location: Location is crucial when investing in real estate. It is important to research and understand the local real estate market, including economic indicators, population growth, and job prospects. Properties in areas with strong economic growth and a growing population are likely to appreciate in value, providing long-term returns on investment.

Property Condition: It is important to assess the condition of the property and make necessary repairs or renovations before putting it on the market. A well-maintained property is more likely to attract tenants and generate a higher rental income.

Financing Options: During a recession, financing options may be limited, and interest rates may be higher. It is important to research and compare financing options to find the best deals and secure funding for property purchases.

Rental Demand: Investing in a property with high rental demand is crucial for generating passive income. Properties in areas with high demand are likely to be more valuable and generate higher rental income.

Timing: Timing is key when investing in real estate. It is important to purchase properties at the right time, taking into account economic indicators and the local real estate market. This requires research and a thorough understanding of the market.

Making Informed Decisions

Investing in real estate during a recession can be a smart move for a common man, but it requires careful consideration and informed decision making. It is important to do thorough research and understand the local real estate market, including economic indicators and population growth. Additionally, it is important to assess the condition of the property, compare financing options, and consider the rental demand of the area.

It is also important to have a long-term perspective when investing in real estate. While the immediate returns may not be significant, a well-researched and well-executed real estate investment can provide long-term financial security and growth.

Conclusion

In conclusion, real estate investments during a recession can be a smart move for a common man. While it requires careful consideration and informed decision making, it can provide opportunities for wealth building and financial security. By understanding the local real estate market, assessing property condition, comparing financing options, and considering rental demand, a common man can make informed decisions and maximize returns on investment.

CHAPTER FIVE

Stock market strategies for a recession

The stock market can be a confusing and intimidating place for many people, especially during a recession when the economy is unstable and uncertainty is high. However, with the right strategies and understanding, the stock market can actually be a valuable tool for building wealth, even in tough economic times. In this essay, we will explore some stock market strategies that are suitable for a common man during a recession.

First, it's important to understand the basics of the stock market. The stock market is essentially a platform for buying and selling stocks, which are ownership units of a company. When you buy a stock, you become a partial owner of the company and have the potential to earn a profit through the company's growth and success. The stock market is influenced by various factors, including economic trends, company performance, and global events.

During a recession, many people are hesitant to invest in the stock market because of concerns about economic instability and market volatility. However, a recession can also provide opportunities for savvy investors to pick up stocks at a discounted price. One strategy is to invest in blue-chip stocks, which are stocks of well-established and financially stable companies with a strong track record of performance. These companies are often less affected by economic downturns and can provide a steady source of income through dividends.

Another strategy is to focus on defensive stocks, which are stocks in industries that are considered to be less affected by economic downturns. For example, stocks in the healthcare and utilities sectors are often seen as defensive because they provide essential services that people need regardless of the state of the economy. Investing in defensive stocks can help reduce risk and provide stability in your portfolio during a recession.

Another approach is to diversify your portfolio by investing in a mix of different stocks and industries. This way, if one industry or company is struggling, your portfolio is less likely to be heavily impacted. It's also a good idea to consider investing in low-cost index funds, which provide exposure to a broad range of stocks and can be a cost-effective way to diversify your portfolio.

Long-term investing is another strategy to consider during a recession. Although the stock market may be volatile in the short-term, over the long-term, it has historically provided a higher rate of return than other investment options such as bonds or savings accounts. By investing for the long-term, you can take advantage of the market's tendency to bounce back over time and potentially earn a higher return on your investment.

It's also important to have a well-thought-out plan for when to sell your stocks. One approach is to use stop-loss orders, which automatically sell your stocks when they reach a certain price. This can help you minimize losses and preserve your capital during a downturn.

Finally, it's crucial to educate yourself and stay informed about the stock market and economic trends. This can help you make informed decisions and stay on top of changes that may impact your investments. There are many resources available, such as financial news websites, online forums, and investment advisors, that can help you stay informed and make the most of your investments during a recession.

In conclusion, investing in the stock market during a recession can be a valuable tool for building wealth, but it's important to have a well-thought-out strategy and stay informed about economic trends and market changes. By investing in blue-chip stocks, defensive stocks, diversifying your portfolio, investing for the long-term, having a plan for when to sell your stocks, and educating yourself, you can potentially increase your chances of success and achieve your financial goals even in challenging economic times.

CHAPTER SIX

Maximizing savings and reducing expenses

Recession can be a stressful time for many people, particularly for those who are trying to build wealth. During a recession, it is common for people to face job loss, reduced income, and a decline in their investment portfolios. While the situation can be challenging, there are several ways to maximize savings and reduce expenses during a recession to help keep your financial situation stable. Here are some tips to help you save money and reduce your expenses during this challenging time.

Make a budget and stick to it. One of the most effective ways to reduce your expenses is to create a budget and stick to it. A budget will help you keep track of your income and expenses and make sure that you are spending within your means. Start by listing all of your fixed expenses, such as rent, utilities, and insurance. Then, add up all of your variable expenses, such as groceries, entertainment, and clothing. Finally, compare your income to your expenses to see if you have any room for saving. If your expenses are higher than your income, you will need to make some changes.

Reduce your housing expenses. Housing is often the largest expense for many people, and during a recession, it may be necessary to find ways to reduce your housing costs. Consider downsizing to a smaller home or apartment, or look for ways to reduce your rent or mortgage payments. You can also save money by making some home improvements, such as adding insulation or upgrading your appliances, which can help reduce your energy bills.

Cut back on entertainment and dining expenses. During a recession, it is essential to reduce your spending on entertainment and dining expenses. This can include cutting back on dining out, reducing your subscription services, and reducing your spending on entertainment, such as movies and concerts. Instead, consider taking advantage of free or low-cost entertainment options, such as public parks, free concerts, and community events.

Reduce transportation costs. Transportation costs can be a significant expense, especially if you drive a car. During a recession, it may be necessary to find ways to reduce your transportation costs. Consider using public transportation, biking, or walking instead of driving. If you must drive, look for ways to reduce your fuel costs, such as carpooling, using public transportation for short trips, or combining trips to reduce the amount of fuel you use.

Shop for bargains. One of the best ways to reduce your expenses is to look for bargains and sales. By shopping for sales and discounts, you can save money on groceries, clothing, and other essential items. Take advantage of discount websites, coupons, and other promotions to get the best deals.

Use cash instead of credit cards. Credit cards can be a significant source of debt, especially during a recession. To reduce your expenses and increase your savings, consider using cash instead of credit cards. This will help you stay within your budget and avoid the temptation of spending money you don't have.

Make use of government assistance programs. If you are facing financial difficulties during a recession, there may be government assistance programs available to help you. Look into programs such as unemployment benefits, food stamps, and energy assistance programs. These programs can provide a valuable source of support during a difficult time.

Start an emergency fund. An emergency fund can provide a source of financial support during a recession, particularly if you lose your job or face unexpected expenses. Start by setting aside a small amount of money each month and gradually increasing the amount over time. This will help you build up a financial cushion that you can rely on in case of an emergency.

In conclusion, a recession can be a challenging time for many people, but by maximizing your savings and

CHAPTER SEVEN

Navigating unemployment and job loss

Navigating Unemployment and Job Loss During a Recession: A Guide for the Common Man

While the effects of a recession can be felt across the board, it is often those in the lower and middle income brackets who are hit hardest. Unemployment and job loss are common occurrences during a recession, leaving many people struggling to make ends meet. However, there are steps that can be taken to navigate this difficult period and come out on the other side with your financial stability intact.

The first step to navigating unemployment and job loss during a recession is to acknowledge that this is a difficult and challenging time. It's important to be kind to yourself, to take care of your physical and emotional well-being, and to be patient. There will likely be a period of adjustment, but it's important to remember that this is temporary and that there are steps you can take to help yourself through this period.

One of the most important things you can do is to be proactive about finding new work. This may involve updating your resume and networking with friends, family members, and colleagues in your field. Utilize online job boards and career websites to search for opportunities and make sure your skills and experience are up to date. Consider looking into industries that are less impacted by the recession or exploring new career paths that may have more job openings.

Another important step is to reduce your expenses as much as possible. Start by creating a budget and making a list of all of your monthly expenses. Look for areas where you can cut back, such as dining out, entertainment, and travel expenses. Consider reducing your monthly bills by negotiating with service providers, such as your cell phone company or cable provider, or by opting for lower cost alternatives. Additionally, consider selling items that you no longer need or use.

It's also a good idea to look into any government assistance programs that may be available to you. Unemployment insurance is a common program that provides financial assistance to those who have lost their jobs. There may also be other programs, such as food assistance, housing assistance, and health insurance subsidies, that can help during this difficult time. Make sure to research all of your options and apply for any programs that you are eligible for.

Another important step is to protect your credit score. Missing payments or defaulting on loans can have a negative impact on your credit score, making it harder to get back on your feet once you do find new work. Consider working with your creditors to arrange a payment plan or, if necessary, consider using a credit counseling service to help manage your debt.

Finally, consider ways to increase your income, even if only temporarily. This may involve taking on freelance work, starting a side business, or taking on a part-time job. This extra income can help to bridge the gap between unemployment and finding new work and can also help to maintain your financial stability during this difficult time.

In conclusion, navigating unemployment and job loss during a recession can be a difficult and challenging time. However, by being proactive, reducing expenses, taking advantage of government assistance programs, protecting your credit score, and finding ways to increase your income, you can help to weather this difficult period and come out on the other side with your financial stability intact. Remember to be kind to yourself, take care of your physical and emotional well-being, and be patient. With determination and a positive attitude, you can navigate this difficult time and come out on the other side stronger and more resilient.

CHAPTER EIGHT

Entrepreneurship in a recession

Entrepreneurship During Recession: A Guide for the Common Man

Recession is a time of economic turmoil, marked by a decline in the Gross Domestic Product (GDP), increased unemployment, and reduced consumer spending. Many people fear recessions and believe that they are not a good time to start a business. However, recessions also present opportunities for entrepreneurs to start new businesses and grow existing ones.

For the common man, entrepreneurship during a recession can be a path to financial stability and independence. By starting a business, a person can control their own financial future, instead of relying on a traditional job that may be affected by the recession. Moreover, recessions often lead to a decrease in competition, as many businesses fail, making it easier for new businesses to establish themselves in the market.

Starting a business during a recession requires careful planning and a clear understanding of the market. It's important to research the industry and identify a niche that has potential for growth, even during a recession. For example, industries that are considered essential, such as healthcare and technology, tend to be less affected by recessions.

When starting a business, it's important to keep costs low. During a recession, customers are more price-sensitive and are looking for bargains. Entrepreneurs should strive to offer high-quality products or services at a lower price than their competitors. This can be achieved by keeping overhead costs low, such as by working from home or outsourcing certain tasks.

Another important aspect of starting a business during a recession is marketing. Entrepreneurs need to make sure that their products or services are well known and accessible to potential customers. This can be done through various marketing channels, such as social media, content marketing, and advertising. It's important to focus on delivering value to customers and building a strong brand, which can help attract and retain customers during and after the recession.

Entrepreneurship during a recession also requires financial discipline. Business owners should keep a tight grip on their finances, avoid overspending, and maintain a healthy cash flow. This means being mindful of expenses and prioritizing the most important expenditures, such as marketing and product development. Entrepreneurs should also have contingency plans in place, in case their business doesn't perform as well as expected, such as cutting costs or finding additional sources of revenue.

Recessions also offer opportunities for existing businesses to grow and expand. For instance, during a recession, companies may be able to acquire struggling businesses at a discounted price. This can be a great way to gain access to new customers, markets, and technologies.

Moreover, businesses can also consider expanding into new markets, as customers may be looking for new products or services during a recession.

In conclusion, entrepreneurship during a recession can be a great opportunity for the common man to take control of their financial future. However, starting and growing a business during a recession requires careful planning, a clear understanding of the market, low costs, effective marketing, financial discipline, and a willingness to adapt and embrace change. By following these principles, entrepreneurs can build successful businesses and create a stable financial future for themselves and their families.

CHAPTER NINE

Leveraging technology to increase income

The global economy has been facing numerous challenges in recent years, with recessions being one of the most impactful. During such times, people tend to lose their jobs or face pay cuts, making it harder for them to make ends meet. This is where technology comes in as a lifesaver. With the advancements in technology, people can use various tools and platforms to increase their income, even during a recession. In this essay, we will explore some of the ways that common people can leverage technology to boost their earnings during economic downturns.

One of the most obvious ways to leverage technology to increase income during a recession is through online freelance work. Platforms such as Upwork, Fiverr, and Freelancer offer an array of opportunities for people to earn money from the comfort of their homes. Freelancing can range from writing, graphic design, coding, to virtual assistance and customer service. These platforms provide an opportunity for people to offer their skills and services to clients from all over the world, thereby increasing their earning potential.

Another way to leverage technology to increase income is through e-commerce. Online marketplaces such as Amazon, Etsy, and eBay offer people an opportunity to start their own businesses and sell products from their homes. These platforms allow individuals to sell items they no longer need or handmade products, thereby providing a source of income during a recession. Additionally, e-commerce platforms offer various tools and resources to help businesses grow and expand, thereby increasing their earning potential.

Technology has also revolutionized the way people save and invest their money. Online platforms such as Robinhood and Stash allow people to invest in stocks and other assets, even with small amounts of money. With these platforms, people can invest in the stock market, real estate, and other assets, thereby growing their wealth and increasing their income. Furthermore, these platforms provide education and resources to help people make informed investment decisions, thereby reducing the risk of losing money.

Technology has also paved the way for passive income streams. Online platforms such as YouTube and Twitch allow people to create content and earn money through advertisements, sponsorships, and other monetization methods. Additionally, people can create digital products such as e-books, courses, and memberships and sell them online, thereby providing a source of passive income. Technology has made it easier for people to reach a global audience, thereby increasing their earning potential.

Lastly, people can leverage technology to save money and reduce expenses. Budgeting and expense tracking apps such as Mint and Personal Capital help people track their spending and find areas where they can reduce their expenses. By reducing their expenses, people can free up more money to invest and increase their income. Technology has also made it easier for people to compare prices and find deals, thereby saving money on purchases and reducing their expenses.

In conclusion, technology has provided numerous opportunities for people to increase their income during a recession. Freelancing, e-commerce, online investing, passive income streams, and expense tracking are just a few of the ways people can leverage technology to boost their earnings. By taking advantage of these tools and platforms, people can increase their financial stability and secure their financial future, even during economic downturns. The key is to continuously educate oneself and stay informed of the latest developments in technology and finance to make the most of these opportunities.

CHAPTER TEN

Alternative sources of income

During times of Recession, it's important to have alternative sources of income to help weather the storm and maintain financial stability. This essay will explore some of the alternative sources of income that are available to the common man during a recession.

Freelancing: One of the simplest ways to earn extra income during a recession is by freelancing. With the rise of the gig economy and the internet, it's easier than ever to find work as a freelancer. Whether you're a graphic designer, writer, web developer, or have other skills, you can offer your services to individuals or companies in need. Websites such as Upwork and Fiverr provide platforms where you can find freelance work and build your portfolio.

Starting a Side Business: Another option for earning additional income during a recession is to start a side business. With low barriers to entry and the ability to start small, a side business can provide a significant source of extra income. Whether you start a home-based business selling handmade goods or offer services such as landscaping or pet-sitting, the opportunities are endless. Just make sure to research and plan your business carefully to ensure success.

Investing: Investing in stocks, bonds, real estate, or other assets can provide an additional source of income during a recession. While investing always comes with risks, during a recession, there may be opportunities to buy assets at a discounted price, providing potential for future gains. It's important to educate yourself on investing and seek professional advice before making any investments.

Renting Out Property: If you own property, such as a spare room, garage, or storage space, you can rent it out for extra income during a recession. Platforms such as Airbnb and storage rental websites can connect you with people in need of additional space, providing a steady stream of passive income.

Selling Goods and Services Online: The rise of e-commerce has made it easier than ever to sell goods and services online. Whether you sell handmade goods on Etsy, offer services through a website, or sell products through Amazon or eBay, the internet provides a platform to reach a global market and earn additional income.

Online Tutoring and Teaching: If you have a skill or knowledge in a particular subject, you can offer your services as an online tutor or teacher. Websites such as Tutor.com and Teachable provide platforms for you to share your knowledge and earn money by teaching others.

Dropshipping: Dropshipping is a business model where you sell products online without holding any inventory. You partner with a supplier who ships products directly to your customers, allowing you to focus on marketing and sales. This model can provide a significant source of extra income, with low start-up costs and the ability to scale quickly.

Affiliate Marketing: Affiliate marketing is a form of advertising where you earn a commission for promoting a product or service. This can be done through a website, blog, or social media, with the potential to earn significant income by promoting products to a large audience.

In conclusion, there are many alternative sources of income available to the common man during a recession. From freelancing and starting a side business to renting out property and selling goods and services online, the opportunities are endless. It's important to research and carefully consider each option to determine which is right for you, and to take the necessary steps to ensure success. With dedication and hard work, these alternative sources of income can provide financial stability and help you thrive during a recession.

CHAPTER ELEVEN

Protecting and growing personal wealth

Recession can be a difficult and challenging time for many people, especially for those who are trying to protect and grow their personal wealth. During a recession, the economy slows down and unemployment rates may rise, making it harder for people to make ends meet and keep their finances in order. However, by understanding the economic dynamics of recessions and making smart financial decisions, it is possible to protect and grow personal wealth even during tough economic times.

The first step in protecting and growing personal wealth during a recession is to understand the economics of recessions. Recessions are characterized by a decline in economic activity, such as a decrease in consumer spending, a rise in unemployment, and a decrease in the production of goods and services. While these factors can make it more difficult to earn money and save, they also create opportunities for those who are prepared and financially savvy. For example, during a recession, real estate prices may drop, making it a good time to buy property, or stocks may become undervalued, providing a buying opportunity for those who are able to invest.

Another key strategy for protecting and growing personal wealth during a recession is to reduce expenses and maximize savings. This can be done by cutting back on non-essential expenses, such as eating out or buying expensive clothing, and by finding ways to save on essential expenses, such as reducing energy costs or shopping for better deals on groceries. Additionally, having an emergency fund with three to six months' worth of living expenses can provide a safety net in case of job loss or other financial emergencies.

One of the most important things that individuals can do to protect and grow their personal wealth during a recession is to focus on increasing their income. This can be done by finding a new job, starting a side business, or leveraging technology to find new sources of income, such as online freelance work or selling goods on websites like Etsy or eBay. Additionally, many people are able to increase their income by taking on extra work or starting a business, such as offering pet-sitting or lawn care services.

Another way to protect and grow personal wealth during a recession is to make smart financial decisions, such as investing in stocks, bonds, or real estate. However, it is important to understand the risks involved in these investments and to do research before investing. Additionally, it may be a good idea to seek the advice of a financial advisor or to attend investment seminars to learn more about investing.

Another key aspect of protecting and growing personal wealth during a recession is to maintain a strong support network. This can include friends, family, or community organizations, who can provide emotional and financial support during difficult times. Additionally, joining a support group, such as a self-help or financial planning group, can provide individuals with the tools and resources they need to improve their finances and grow their personal wealth.

Finally, it is important to stay educated and informed about finance and economics during a recession. This can be done by reading books, attending seminars, or taking online courses to learn more about personal finance and investment strategies. By continuously educating oneself, individuals can stay ahead of the curve and be better prepared to protect and grow their personal wealth during tough economic times.

In conclusion, protecting and growing personal wealth during a recession is possible with a combination of smart financial decisions, reducing expenses, maximizing savings, increasing income, making informed investments, building a strong support network, and staying educated and informed about finance and economics. By following these strategies, individuals can weather the storms of a recession and come out stronger on the other side.

CHAPTER TWELVE

Taking calculated financial risks

Taking Calculated Financial Risks During Recession: An Essay for the Common Man

Recession is a challenging time for everyone, but it can be particularly difficult for the common man who may not have the financial resources or expertise to navigate the uncertain economic climate. While it's natural to feel nervous and cautious during a recession, it's important to remember that it can also present opportunities for financial growth and stability. By taking calculated financial risks, the common man can not only weather the recession but also come out on the other side in a better financial position.

The first step in taking calculated financial risks during a recession is to understand the economic climate and identify opportunities. During a recession, many businesses may be struggling, but others may be expanding as they take advantage of market dislocations and seek to capitalize on new opportunities. For the common man, this could mean investing in a start-up or considering alternative investments such as real estate or stocks. However, it's important to carefully research these options and seek advice from trusted financial experts to ensure that the risks are understood and manageable.

Another important factor to consider when taking calculated financial risks during a recession is personal financial stability. It's essential to have a strong emergency fund in place to help weather any financial setbacks, as well as to be mindful of expenses and look for ways to reduce costs. This could mean cutting back on unnecessary expenses, negotiating bills, or finding alternative sources of income such as freelance work or starting a side business.

In addition to being mindful of personal financial stability, it's also important to be strategic when it comes to investing. During a recession, the stock market may be volatile, and it's essential to understand the risks involved in investing in stocks and other financial products. A common man can seek out low-cost index funds or exchange-traded funds (ETFs), which can provide exposure to a wide range of stocks and help to reduce risk. It's also important to be patient and not make hasty decisions, as the stock market is likely to recover over time.

Another key aspect of taking calculated financial risks during a recession is being financially agile. This means being prepared to adapt to changing circumstances and being willing to take advantage of new opportunities as they arise. For example, if the common man has invested in a start-up that is struggling during a recession, they may need to consider cutting their losses and seeking out new investment opportunities. By being financially agile, the common man can stay ahead of the curve and take advantage of opportunities as they arise.

Finally, it's important for the common man to have a strong support network when taking calculated financial risks during a recession. This could include family, friends, financial advisors, or online communities. By seeking out support and advice from trusted sources, the common man can stay informed and make informed decisions about their finances.

In conclusion, taking calculated financial risks during a recession can be a daunting prospect, but it can also be an opportunity for the common man to build financial stability and grow their wealth. By understanding the economic climate, being mindful of personal financial stability, being strategic in investments, being financially agile, and having a strong support network, the common man can take advantage of opportunities and weather the challenges of a recession.

CHAPTER THIRTEEN

Understanding and managing debt

Debt is a double-edged sword – it can either be a tool for financial growth or a burden that weighs down your future. During a recession, managing debt becomes even more critical as economic conditions can impact your ability to pay off debts and create new ones. Understanding debt and managing it effectively during a recession is crucial for the financial well-being of any individual. In this essay, we will explore the various types of debt, the impact of a recession on debt management, and practical strategies for managing debt during tough economic times.

Types of Debt: Debt can be categorized into two broad categories – secured and unsecured. Secured debt is a debt that is backed by collateral, such as a mortgage or a car loan. Unsecured debt, on the other hand, is a debt that is not backed by collateral, such as credit card debt or personal loans. It is important to understand the differences between these two types of debt as the impact of a recession on each can be different.

Impact of Recession on Debt Management: During a recession, employment rates decline, businesses fail, and disposable income decreases, making it more difficult for individuals to make their debt payments. This, in turn, can lead to an increase in default rates, making it more difficult for individuals to obtain credit in the future. Additionally, the recession can cause a decrease in the value of assets, such as homes, which can make it more difficult to use them as collateral for loans.

Practical Strategies for Managing Debt during a Recession:

- Prioritize Debt Repayment: The first step in managing debt during a recession is to prioritize debt repayment. This means making minimum payments on all debts, while focusing extra payments on the debt with the highest interest rate.
- Create a Budget: Creating a budget is a crucial step in managing debt during a recession. A budget will help you understand your income and expenses and help you allocate funds to pay off debt.
- Negotiate with Creditors: If you are having difficulty making debt payments, reach out to your creditors to negotiate a new payment plan. This could involve extending the term of the loan or reducing the monthly payment amount.
- Seek Professional Help: If your debt situation becomes unmanageable, consider seeking professional help from a financial advisor or a credit counseling agency. These organizations can help you develop a debt management plan and negotiate with your creditors on your behalf.
- Avoid New Debt: During a recession, it is crucial to avoid taking on new debt. Instead, focus on paying off existing debt and building up an emergency fund to help you through tough times.

- Take Advantage of Low Interest Rates: If interest rates are low, consider refinancing your debt to reduce your monthly payments or to pay off debt faster.

Conclusion: Debt is a complex issue, and managing it during a recession can be challenging. However, by prioritizing debt repayment, creating a budget, negotiating with creditors, seeking professional help, avoiding new debt, and taking advantage of low interest rates, individuals can effectively manage their debt and protect their financial future. In uncertain economic times, it is important to stay disciplined, focused, and informed to ensure financial stability and security.

CHAPTER FOURTEEN

The psychology of wealth building

The Psychology of Wealth Building during a Recession

A recession is a period of economic downturn characterized by a decline in gross domestic product (GDP), high unemployment rates, and reduced consumer spending. During these times, it can be challenging to build wealth, but it is not impossible. Building wealth during a recession requires a combination of financial literacy, discipline, and a growth mindset. However, perhaps the most critical factor is the psychology of wealth building, as the way we think about money and wealth can have a significant impact on our ability to build and maintain it.

The first step to building wealth during a recession is to have a growth mindset. This means having an open and optimistic outlook, believing that financial challenges can be overcome and opportunities can be found. People with a growth mindset see setbacks and failures as opportunities for growth and learning, rather than as permanent barriers to success. This kind of attitude is crucial during a recession, as it allows individuals to stay focused on their long-term financial goals and not be discouraged by short-term challenges.

Another critical aspect of the psychology of wealth building during a recession is the need to develop financial literacy. Financial literacy refers to having the knowledge and skills necessary to make informed and responsible financial decisions. This includes understanding basic financial concepts such as budgeting, saving, investing, and debt management. Financial literacy is crucial in a recession, as it allows individuals to understand their financial situation, identify opportunities to build wealth, and make informed decisions about their finances.

In addition to having a growth mindset and financial literacy, discipline is also crucial in building wealth during a recession. Discipline means being consistent in following a financial plan, making informed decisions about spending and investing, and sticking to a budget. It also means avoiding impulsive or emotionally driven financial decisions and avoiding debt when possible.

Fear and uncertainty are common during a recession, but it is important to remember that fear is often irrational and can lead to poor financial decisions. For example, many people may be tempted to sell their investments during a market downturn, but this can be a costly mistake. A better approach is to have a long-term perspective, understand the market cycles, and focus on building a diversified portfolio.

Moreover, networking and building partnerships can also play a crucial role in building wealth during a recession. This means reaching out to others in your industry or network and forming strategic alliances that can help you access new opportunities and resources. Networking can also help you stay informed about new trends and changes in the market, allowing you to make more informed decisions about your finances.

Finally, it is important to have a strong support network during a recession. This includes friends, family, and a financial advisor or mentor who can provide guidance, support, and encouragement during challenging times. Having a strong support network can help you stay focused on your financial goals and maintain a positive outlook, even during difficult times.

In conclusion, building wealth during a recession requires a combination of financial literacy, discipline, and a growth mindset. The psychology of wealth building is critical in this process, as the way we think about money and wealth can have a significant impact on our ability to build and maintain it. By developing a growth mindset, financial literacy, discipline, and a strong support network, individuals can overcome the challenges of a recession and build long-term wealth.

CHAPTER FIFTEEN

Building a strong support network

Building a strong support network during a recession is an essential aspect of surviving and thriving in tough economic times. A recession can bring on a range of challenges, including job loss, reduced income, and financial stress, which can be difficult to overcome without the support of others. This essay will provide tips for common people on how to build a strong support network during a recession, and why it is so important.

One of the first steps to building a strong support network during a recession is to identify who is already in your network. This includes friends, family, colleagues, and acquaintances. Reach out to those people and see if they are open to providing support, whether it's through lending an ear, offering advice, or lending money if necessary. It's also important to cultivate new relationships with people who may be in a similar situation, or who have faced similar challenges in the past. Joining support groups, attending networking events, and participating in community activities are all ways to make new connections.

It is also important to have a clear understanding of what kind of support you need. For example, you may need help with childcare, finding a job, or managing finances. Once you have a clear understanding of what kind of support you need, you can be more proactive in seeking out individuals or organizations that can provide that support.

Another key aspect of building a strong support network is to be open and honest about your situation. Sharing your struggles with others can help you feel less isolated and more connected to others. It can also help you build trust with others and establish a sense of accountability. This can be especially beneficial for people who are feeling stressed or overwhelmed. When you share your struggles with others, you are giving them an opportunity to help, and they are more likely to do so if they feel they understand what you are going through.

It is also important to be open to receiving help from others. This may mean accepting monetary donations, accepting help with household chores, or accepting emotional support. It can be tempting to try to handle everything on your own, but accepting help from others can be a valuable way to reduce stress and improve your overall well-being.

In addition to building a strong support network, it is also important to take care of your mental and physical health. This can be done by engaging in self-care activities, such as exercise, meditation, or hobbies. It is also important to eat well and get enough sleep. Taking care of yourself will help you stay focused and motivated, and will make it easier to cope with the challenges of a recession.

Finally, it is important to be proactive in building your support network, even before a recession hits. Building relationships with others and establishing a strong support network will help you be better prepared for a downturn, and will make it easier to get through the tough times.

In conclusion, building a strong support network during a recession is a critical component of surviving and thriving in tough economic times. By identifying who is already in your network, cultivating new relationships, being open and honest about your situation, and taking care of your mental and physical health, you can build a strong support network that will help you through the tough times. Remember, you don't have to go through a recession alone - reach out to others and allow them to support you in your journey.

CHAPTER SIXTEEN

Continuously educating yourself financially

Financial literacy is a crucial component of building and maintaining wealth. In difficult economic times such as recessions, it becomes even more important to continuously educate oneself financially in order to weather the storm. By understanding the basics of finance and economics, one can make informed decisions about their money and investments, ultimately increasing their chances of success in the long run.

There are a variety of ways to continuously educate oneself financially during a recession. One of the most accessible and cost-effective ways is to read books and articles about finance and economics. A wealth of information is available online for free, including articles, blog posts, and e-books, making it easy to expand one's knowledge on a variety of financial topics.

Another way to educate oneself financially during a recession is to take advantage of free resources offered by government agencies and non-profit organizations. The Federal Reserve Bank, for example, offers a range of educational resources on their website, including articles and videos on various financial topics. Additionally, non-profit organizations like the National Endowment for Financial Education (NEFE) provide a range of resources and tools to help individuals better understand personal finance.

Online courses and webinars are also a great way to continuously educate oneself financially. Many online platforms offer courses and webinars that are specifically focused on finance and economics, and these can be taken at any time, from anywhere in the world. Online courses can be especially beneficial for individuals who may have limited access to traditional financial education resources due to geographic location or time constraints.

Another effective way to educate oneself financially during a recession is to seek out mentors and seek advice from those who have experience and expertise in finance and economics. This can include financial advisors, accountants, or even friends and family members who have a strong understanding of personal finance. These individuals can offer valuable insights and guidance, helping to fill in any gaps in one's financial knowledge.

It is also important to keep up-to-date with the latest financial news and economic trends. Following financial news sources, such as the Wall Street Journal or CNBC, and attending financial seminars or workshops can help individuals stay informed about changes in the economy and learn about new financial strategies and products.

Finally, being proactive about financial planning during a recession is a key way to continuously educate oneself financially. This means having a clear understanding of one's income, expenses, debts, and assets, and creating a budget and investment plan that aligns with one's financial goals. Engaging in regular financial planning helps individuals to stay focused on their goals and make informed financial decisions, even in the midst of economic turmoil.

In conclusion, continuously educating oneself financially during a recession is a crucial step in building and maintaining wealth. By taking advantage of free resources, seeking mentorship and advice, staying informed about the latest financial news and trends, and being proactive about financial planning, individuals can make informed decisions about their money and investments, increasing their chances of financial success in the long run.

CHAPTER SEVENTEEN

Developing a long-term financial plan

Developing a long-term financial plan during a recession is crucial for anyone looking to secure their financial future and weather the economic storm. A recession is a period of economic decline characterized by decreased gross domestic product (GDP), high unemployment, and a decrease in consumer spending. It can have a significant impact on personal finances, making it essential to have a solid financial plan in place. This essay will discuss the steps that a common man can take to develop a long-term financial plan during a recession.

Step 1: Assess Your Current Financial Situation The first step in developing a financial plan is to understand your current financial situation. This includes reviewing your income, expenses, debts, and assets. It's important to know exactly how much money you have coming in each month and how much you are spending on various expenses. By doing this, you will have a better understanding of your current financial position and be able to identify areas where you can make changes.

Step 2: Establish Financial Goals Once you have assessed your current financial situation, it's time to establish your financial goals. This includes both short-term and long-term goals. Your short-term goals could include paying off high-interest debt, building an emergency fund, or saving for a down payment on a home. Long-term goals could include saving for retirement, paying for your children's education, or buying a vacation home. Be sure to set realistic and attainable goals that align with your values and priorities.

Step 3: Create a Budget The next step is to create a budget that reflects your financial goals and current financial situation. A budget will help you control your spending and ensure that you have enough money to meet your financial obligations and reach your financial goals. Be sure to allocate a portion of your income to savings and debt repayment, and track your spending to ensure you are staying on track.

Step 4: Reduce Expenses Reducing expenses is an essential component of a financial plan during a recession. This may involve cutting back on luxury items, shopping for discounts, and looking for ways to save on essential expenses, such as utilities and groceries. Consider negotiating with service providers for better rates and exploring alternative options, such as using public transportation instead of driving.

Step 5: Increase Income Increasing your income is another way to improve your financial situation during a recession. This could include taking on a part-time job, starting a side business, or selling assets that are no longer needed. It's important to consider your skills and interests when looking for ways to increase your income.

Step 6: Invest Wisely Investing is a crucial component of a long-term financial plan. During a recession, it's important to choose investments that are less risky and have the potential for steady growth. This could include bonds, mutual funds, and index funds. Be sure to do your research and consult with a financial advisor before making any investment decisions.

Step 7: Protect Your Financial Future Finally, it's important to protect your financial future by having a solid emergency fund, adequate insurance coverage, and a will. An emergency fund is a savings account that should be used to cover unexpected expenses, such as a job loss or medical emergency. Adequate insurance coverage will protect you and your family in the event of an unexpected event, such as a serious illness or accident. A will ensures that your assets will be distributed according to your wishes after you pass away.

In conclusion, developing a long-term financial plan during a recession is crucial for anyone looking to secure their financial future. The steps outlined in this essay can help you assess your current financial situation, establish financial goals, create a budget, reduce expenses, increase income, invest wisely, and protect your financial

CHAPTER EIGHTEEN

Staying disciplined and focused on goals

Staying disciplined and focused on goals during a recession can be a challenging task for the average person. However, with the right mindset and approach, anyone can weather this economic storm and come out even stronger. A recession is a difficult time for everyone, but it also presents opportunities for those who are prepared and have a plan in place.

The first step to staying disciplined during a recession is to have a clear understanding of your financial situation. This means knowing your income, expenses, debts, and assets. With this information, you can develop a realistic budget that takes into account the economic downturn and helps you stay on track with your financial goals. Additionally, it is important to track your spending and make adjustments as needed to ensure that you are living within your means.

Next, it is important to focus on your goals and remain disciplined in pursuing them. This might mean making sacrifices and saying no to certain expenses that are not essential. For example, you may need to cut back on dining out or entertainment expenses in order to stay within your budget. By focusing on your goals, you can avoid the temptation to overspend and stay on track with your financial plan.

One of the biggest challenges during a recession is job loss or unemployment. If this happens to you, it is important to remain focused on your goals and continue to work towards financial stability. This might mean taking a temporary job, starting a side business, or exploring alternative sources of income. Whatever your situation, staying disciplined and focused on your goals will help you get through this difficult time and come out on the other side in a better financial position.

Another important aspect of staying disciplined during a recession is to continue to educate yourself financially. This might mean reading books, attending workshops, or seeking advice from a financial advisor. By staying informed, you will be better equipped to make informed decisions and navigate the challenges of a recession.

Building a strong support network can also be helpful during a recession. Surrounding yourself with positive, supportive individuals who understand your goals and offer encouragement can help keep you motivated and focused. Additionally, having a trusted friend or family member who can offer financial advice can be invaluable during this difficult time.

Finally, it is important to be prepared for the next recession by building a solid financial foundation. This might mean increasing your savings, paying off debt, and investing in your future. By taking these steps now, you will be better positioned to weather the next economic downturn and continue pursuing your financial goals.

In conclusion, staying disciplined and focused on your goals during a recession is not easy, but it is possible. By having a clear understanding of your financial situation, focusing on your goals, continuing to educate yourself, building a strong support network, and being prepared for the next recession, anyone can weather this economic storm and come out stronger. Remember, a recession is a time of challenge, but it is also a time of opportunity. By staying disciplined and focused on your goals, you can take advantage of this opportunity and build a better financial future for yourself and your family.

CHAPTER NINETEEN

Building multiple streams of income

Building multiple streams of income during a recession is a crucial step for financial stability and security. With a single source of income, you put all your eggs in one basket, making you vulnerable to job loss or pay cuts during an economic downturn. On the other hand, having multiple streams of income can help you weather the storm and even thrive during a recession. In this essay, we will discuss the benefits of building multiple streams of income, ways to create additional income streams, and tips for making the most of them during a recession.

The primary benefit of having multiple streams of income is increased financial security. During a recession, many people experience job loss or pay cuts, making it difficult to make ends meet. However, having other sources of income can help cushion the blow, as well as provide a sense of security and peace of mind. Additionally, having multiple streams of income can increase your overall earning potential, helping you to save more, pay off debt, and reach financial goals faster.

To build multiple streams of income, you first need to identify your strengths and skills, and then determine the best way to monetize them. There are many different ways to create additional income streams, including starting a side business, freelancing, investing, or renting out property. The key is to find something that you are passionate about, as well as something that can generate a steady, reliable income.

Starting a side business is a popular option for building multiple streams of income. Whether it's a service-based business or a product-based business, starting a side hustle allows you to leverage your skills and experience to create an additional source of income. When starting a side business, it's important to have a solid business plan, a clear understanding of your target market, and a commitment to making the business successful. Additionally, it's a good idea to start small and scale up as the business grows, as this will help minimize risk and increase your chances of success.

Freelancing is another great way to build multiple streams of income. Whether you're a graphic designer, writer, or marketer, freelancing allows you to leverage your skills and experience to create a flexible and scalable source of income. There are many online platforms, such as Upwork and Fiverr, that connect freelancers with clients, making it easier than ever to get started. When freelancing, it's important to set clear expectations with clients, maintain a professional demeanor, and deliver quality work consistently.

Investing is another popular way to build multiple streams of income. Whether you're investing in stocks, real estate, or a small business, investing allows you to generate passive income and grow your wealth over time. When investing, it's important to do your research, understand the risks involved, and have a clear understanding of your goals and risk tolerance. Additionally, it's important to diversify your investments, as this will help minimize risk and maximize returns.

Renting out property is another option for building multiple streams of income. Whether it's a spare room in your home or a rental property, renting out property can provide a steady source of passive income. When renting out property, it's important to understand the laws and regulations involved, have a clear understanding of your target market, and have a solid plan for managing the property. Additionally, it's important to have a clear understanding of your expenses and potential returns, as this will help you make informed decisions about renting out property.

Finally, to make the most of multiple streams of income during a recession, it's important to have a clear understanding of your financial goals and priorities. This will help you focus on the most

CHAPTER TWENTY

Being prepared for the next recession

Recession is a normal part of the economic cycle and occurs when the economy experiences a slowdown. It can be triggered by several factors such as a decline in consumer spending, a drop in housing prices, or a decline in the stock market. In a recession, businesses tend to suffer as demand for their goods and services decreases. Unemployment rates rise, and many people struggle to make ends meet. It is important for everyone, especially the common man, to be prepared for the next recession. Here are some tips to help you weather the storm and come out on the other side financially stable.

Build an emergency fund: An emergency fund is a savings account that you can use to cover unexpected expenses, such as a job loss or medical emergency. Aim to have enough money in this account to cover your living expenses for at least three to six months. This will give you time to find another source of income if you lose your job or need to take time off work for medical reasons.

Reduce debt: Debt can quickly become a burden during a recession, making it difficult to make ends meet. Reduce your debt as much as possible before the next recession hits. This may mean paying off credit card balances, car loans, and other types of debt.

Diversify your investments: Diversification is key when it comes to investing. Spread your investments across different asset classes, such as stocks, bonds, and real estate. This way, if one asset class performs poorly, you won't lose all your money. Consider working with a financial advisor to develop a well-diversified investment strategy.

Stay informed: Keeping up with current events and economic news can help you make informed decisions about your finances. Stay informed about changes in the economy and be prepared to adjust your financial strategy as needed.

Consider alternative sources of income: In a recession, it can be difficult to find a job or make ends meet. Consider alternative sources of income, such as freelance work or starting a side business. This way, you'll have a backup plan in case your primary source of income is affected.

Stay disciplined: It can be tempting to splurge during a recession, but it's important to stay disciplined with your spending. Stick to a budget and prioritize saving over spending. This will help you stay afloat during tough times.

Be proactive: Don't wait until the recession hits to start making changes to your finances. Take steps now to prepare for the next recession. This could mean building an emergency fund, reducing debt, or finding alternative sources of income.

In conclusion, being prepared for the next recession is important for everyone, especially the common man. By taking steps to prepare now, you can weather the storm and come out on the other side financially stable. Remember to build an emergency fund, reduce debt, diversify your investments, stay informed, consider alternative sources of income, stay disciplined, and be proactive. With these steps, you can be confident in your ability to handle the next recession and emerge stronger on the other side.

CHAPTER TWENTY-ONE

Making smart and informed financial decisions

Making smart and informed financial decisions during a recession is crucial for everyone, not just wealthy individuals. While a recession can be a time of uncertainty and insecurity, it also presents opportunities for those who are prepared. By understanding the economics of recessions and developing a strong financial foundation, you can protect your wealth and even grow it during tough times. Here are some tips for making smart and informed financial decisions during a recession.

Building an emergency fund: The first step in preparing for a recession is building an emergency fund. This fund should be enough to cover your expenses for at least three to six months. Having this cushion in place will provide peace of mind and reduce financial stress during a downturn.

Understanding your expenses: Knowing your expenses is essential for making informed financial decisions. By tracking your spending and identifying areas where you can reduce costs, you can free up more money to put towards your emergency fund or other investments.

Reducing debt: High levels of debt can be a major burden during a recession, as it reduces your financial flexibility. To prepare, focus on paying off high-interest debt, such as credit card balances, and avoid taking on new debt.

Diversifying your investments: Diversifying your investments is a key strategy for protecting your wealth during a recession. This means spreading your investments across different types of assets, such as stocks, bonds, real estate, and commodities. By diversifying, you can reduce the risk of losing your entire portfolio in a single market downturn.

Staying informed: Staying informed about the latest economic news and trends is important for making smart financial decisions during a recession. Read news articles, watch financial news programs, and consider working with a financial advisor to stay up-to-date on the latest developments.

Identifying opportunities: Recessions can present opportunities for those who are prepared. For example, you may be able to purchase real estate at a discounted price, invest in stocks at lower prices, or start a business in a growing industry. Look for opportunities that align with your financial goals and invest in them.

Building multiple streams of income: During a recession, it's important to have multiple sources of income to provide financial stability. Consider starting a side business, freelancing, or finding additional part-time work to supplement your main income.

Making use of government assistance programs: If you are struggling financially during a recession, you may be eligible for government assistance programs, such as unemployment benefits, food assistance, and housing subsidies. Do some research to determine what programs you may be eligible for and apply for them if needed.

Planning for the long-term: Making smart financial decisions during a recession means planning for the long-term, not just for the short-term. This means developing a budget, saving for retirement, and investing in your future. Consider setting financial goals and creating a plan to achieve them, even during tough economic times.

Seeking professional advice: Finally, consider working with a financial advisor if you're unsure about how to handle your finances during a recession. A financial advisor can provide personalized advice, help you understand your options, and provide a strategic plan for growing your wealth.

In conclusion, a recession can be a challenging time, but with careful planning and informed decision-making, you can protect your wealth and even grow it. Focus on building an emergency fund, reducing debt, diversifying your investments, staying informed, and seeking professional advice. By following these tips, you'll be better prepared to navigate the challenges of a recession and come out stronger on the other side.

CHAPTER TWENTY-TWO

Taking advantage of market dislocations

Taking advantage of market dislocations during a recession can be a valuable strategy for a common man to grow his wealth. A market dislocation occurs when the prices of assets deviate from their fair value, creating opportunities for investors to buy low and sell high. While a recession is often characterized by economic uncertainty and instability, it can also present opportunities for those who are prepared and willing to take advantage of market dislocations.

The key to successfully taking advantage of market dislocations during a recession is to have a solid understanding of the market and the assets you are investing in. It is important to have a long-term perspective, as well as the patience and discipline to wait for the right opportunities to arise. Additionally, it is important to diversify your investments, so that you are not overly exposed to any one asset class or market sector.

One of the most effective ways to take advantage of market dislocations during a recession is to invest in undervalued assets. This can include stocks, bonds, real estate, or other types of investments that have fallen in value due to economic or market conditions. For example, during a recession, the stock market may experience a significant drop, leading to an increase in the prices of certain stocks that are considered to be undervalued. By investing in these stocks, you can take advantage of the market dislocation and potentially realize significant gains in the long run.

Another way to take advantage of market dislocations during a recession is to invest in alternative assets. Alternative assets can include real estate, commodities, and private equity, among others. These types of assets are not as closely tied to the stock market and may provide a hedge against economic uncertainty. For example, during a recession, real estate may be a more attractive investment option compared to stocks, as real estate prices tend to be more stable in times of economic uncertainty.

In addition to investing in undervalued assets and alternative investments, it is also important to be aware of government policies and programs that may be available during a recession. For example, during the recent economic recession, the government provided various forms of financial support, such as low-interest loans, to businesses and individuals. By taking advantage of these programs, you can potentially increase your financial stability during a time of uncertainty.

However, it is also important to be cautious when taking advantage of market dislocations during a recession. While the potential for profit may be high, there is also the risk of loss. It is important to thoroughly research and understand the assets you are investing in, and to have a solid understanding of the market conditions. Additionally, it is important to have a well-diversified portfolio, so that you are not overly exposed to any one asset class or market sector.

In conclusion, taking advantage of market dislocations during a recession can be a valuable strategy for a common man to grow his wealth. By investing in undervalued assets, alternative investments, and taking advantage of government policies, a common man can potentially realize significant gains in the long run. However, it is important to be cautious, thoroughly research the assets you are investing in, and have a well-diversified portfolio in order to minimize risk and maximize potential gains.

CHAPTER TWENTY-THREE

Networking and building partnerships

Networking and building partnerships are crucial aspects of personal and professional growth, but they become even more important during economic downturns such as a recession. In such times, it is not uncommon for businesses to face financial difficulties and for individuals to lose their jobs, but the right connections and partnerships can help weather the storm and even lead to new opportunities for growth.

For the average person, building a strong network and establishing partnerships can seem like a daunting task, especially during a recession. However, it is possible to effectively network and build partnerships, even for those who are not naturally outgoing or confident. The key is to start small, be proactive, and continually build relationships over time.

One of the first steps in building a strong network is to identify potential connections. This can include friends, family members, colleagues, acquaintances, and even members of online communities who share similar interests. When identifying potential connections, it is important to look for individuals who have common goals, values, and interests, as these are the relationships that are most likely to flourish.

Once you have identified potential connections, it is important to take the initiative and reach out to them. This can be done through a variety of methods, including email, phone calls, in-person meetings, or even social media. When reaching out, it is important to be genuine, polite, and respectful, as these qualities can help establish trust and open doors for future opportunities.

Networking events can also be a great way to meet new people and build relationships. These events can include industry-specific conferences, trade shows, and even local meetups. When attending these events, it is important to be proactive, engage with others, and participate in discussions. This can help establish new connections and even lead to future opportunities for collaboration.

Building partnerships, on the other hand, involves taking the relationships established through networking to the next level. This can include forming business partnerships, joint ventures, or even mentorship relationships. When building partnerships, it is important to ensure that both parties have complementary skills, resources, and goals. This can help ensure that the partnership is beneficial for both parties and can lead to long-term success.

One of the key benefits of partnerships during a recession is that they can help spread the risk and provide support during difficult times. For example, a business partnership can help ensure that the workload is shared and that there is someone to turn to when challenges arise. This can help keep businesses afloat and provide a sense of stability during uncertain times.

Partnerships can also help individuals access new resources and opportunities that they may not have had access to on their own. For example, a mentor-mentee relationship can provide guidance and support to help individuals reach their goals, while a business partnership can help expand reach and access to new markets.

In conclusion, networking and building partnerships are essential skills that can help individuals and businesses thrive during a recession. By identifying potential connections, taking the initiative to reach out, and continuously building relationships over time, individuals can establish a strong network that can provide support and lead to new opportunities for growth. Building partnerships can help spread the risk, provide support, and access new resources and opportunities, helping individuals and businesses weather the storm during a recession and emerge even stronger.

CHAPTER TWENTY-FOUR

Making use of government assistance programs

Making use of government assistance programs during a recession is a smart financial strategy for the common man. During tough economic times, many people are struggling to make ends meet and pay their bills. However, the government provides various programs to help individuals and families get through these tough times. The following essay will explain the different types of government assistance programs that are available and how to take advantage of them.

One of the most well-known government assistance programs is unemployment insurance. This program provides temporary financial assistance to those who have lost their job through no fault of their own. Unemployment insurance can provide a source of income while individuals are searching for a new job. It is important to note that unemployment insurance is only available to those who have been employed for a certain amount of time, so it is important to check with your state's Department of Labor to see if you are eligible.

Another government assistance program that is available during a recession is the Supplemental Nutrition Assistance Program (SNAP). This program helps low-income families purchase food. The assistance is provided in the form of an Electronic Benefits Transfer (EBT) card, which works like a debit card. SNAP is a great program for those who are struggling to make ends meet, as it can provide a significant source of assistance with food expenses.

The Low Income Home Energy Assistance Program (LIHEAP) is a government assistance program that provides financial assistance to low-income families to help with heating and cooling expenses. This program is especially important during a recession, as many families may be struggling to pay their bills due to a reduction in income. LIHEAP provides financial assistance to help families pay their energy bills, so they can stay warm in the winter and cool in the summer.

The Temporary Assistance for Needy Families (TANF) program is another government assistance program that is available during a recession. This program provides temporary financial assistance to families who are struggling to make ends meet. TANF provides a source of income for families who are in need, and it can also provide job training and other support services to help individuals get back on their feet.

One of the most important things to remember when making use of government assistance programs is to apply as soon as possible. Many programs have limited funding and are first come, first served. It is also important to be prepared with the required documentation, such as proof of income, and to provide accurate information on your application.

In conclusion, the government provides various programs to help individuals and families get through tough economic times. Unemployment insurance, SNAP, LIHEAP, and TANF are just a few of the programs available to those in need. Making use of these programs can provide a source of income and support during a recession, and it is important to apply as soon as possible to take advantage of these resources. By taking advantage of government assistance programs, the common man can weather the storm of a recession and get back on the path to financial stability.

CHAPTER TWENTY-FIVE

Finding and securing steady passive income sources

Finding and securing steady passive income sources during a recession can be a challenge for many people, but it is possible with some effort and research. A recession is a period of economic decline characterized by decreased consumer spending, high unemployment, and a general decrease in economic activity. During a recession, it becomes more important than ever to have a reliable source of passive income to help you weather the economic storm.

Passive income is income that is earned without the need for active involvement or work. Some common examples of passive income sources include rental properties, dividend-paying stocks, and interest from savings accounts. The beauty of passive income is that it provides a steady stream of revenue without the need for constant work, making it an ideal way to generate income during a recession.

To find and secure passive income sources, the first step is to assess your financial situation. This includes understanding your current income, expenses, and debts. This information will help you determine how much money you can realistically allocate towards passive income investments.

Next, you should research and consider different passive income streams that align with your financial goals, risk tolerance, and available capital. For example, if you have a low risk tolerance, you might consider investing in a savings account or certificate of deposit. If you are willing to take on a little more risk, you might consider investing in dividend-paying stocks or rental properties.

Investing in rental properties is one of the most popular ways to generate passive income. This involves purchasing a property, either by taking out a loan or using your own savings, and renting it out to tenants. The rental income you earn can provide a steady stream of passive income, and property values have historically tended to appreciate over time, providing the potential for long-term growth. However, it's important to consider that being a landlord also involves responsibilities such as property maintenance, finding and managing tenants, and navigating local regulations.

Another option for generating passive income is to invest in dividend-paying stocks. Dividend stocks are shares of a company that pay a portion of the company's profits to its shareholders on a regular basis. Investing in dividend stocks can provide a steady stream of passive income, and it also has the potential for long-term growth through stock price appreciation.

If you have a large sum of money saved up, you might consider investing in a peer-to-peer lending platform, such as Lending Club or Prosper. Peer-to-peer lending involves lending money to individuals or small businesses and earning interest on your investment. This can provide a steady stream of passive income, but it also involves risk, as there is always a possibility of default.

It is also possible to generate passive income through creating and selling digital products, such as e-books or courses. This involves creating a product once, and then selling it over and over again without the need for additional effort. This is a great option for those with expertise in a particular area and can be a good source of passive income if done correctly.

In conclusion, finding and securing steady passive income sources during a recession requires research, planning, and a willingness to take on some risk. However, the effort invested can pay off in the long run, providing a reliable source of income that can help you weather an economic downturn. It's important to assess your financial situation, research different passive income streams, and invest in sources that align with your financial goals, risk tolerance, and available capital. By doing so, you can increase your financial stability during a recession and put yourself in a better position for long-term financial success.

CHAPTER TWENTY-SIX

Making informed and strategic investments

Making informed and strategic investments during a recession can be a difficult task for a common man, as the economic downturn can cause uncertainty and fear in the market. However, with the right approach and mindset, it is possible to turn a recession into a profitable opportunity. In this essay, we will discuss the importance of education and research, the benefits of a diversified portfolio, and the key principles to follow when making investments during a recession.

First, education and research are crucial for making informed investment decisions. Before making any investment, it is important to educate oneself about the current market conditions, the different investment options available, and their potential returns and risks. A common man should also be aware of the various economic indicators, such as interest rates and inflation, which can impact their investments. Moreover, it is important to keep up to date with the latest news and events that may affect the market, such as changes in government policies, mergers, and acquisitions.

One of the most effective ways to mitigate the risks associated with investing during a recession is to diversify one's portfolio. By spreading investments across different asset classes, such as stocks, bonds, real estate, and commodities, a common man can reduce the overall risk of their portfolio and improve its stability. Diversification also helps to spread the impact of market fluctuations, so that if one investment performs poorly, others may still provide returns. Additionally, investing in different sectors, such as technology, healthcare, and consumer goods, can also help to reduce risk and improve the chances of earning a profit.

When making investments during a recession, it is important to follow a set of key principles to ensure success. Firstly, it is important to maintain a long-term perspective. While short-term market fluctuations may cause panic, it is important to remember that recessions are typically temporary and that the market will eventually recover. Secondly, it is important to be patient and avoid making impulsive decisions based on short-term market movements. Instead, a common man should take a calculated approach and make investment decisions based on sound analysis and research.

Another important principle is to avoid chasing after quick profits. Instead, a common man should focus on steady and consistent returns, which can be achieved through smart investments in undervalued assets. Additionally, it is important to have a clear understanding of one's financial goals and risk tolerance, and to align investments with these objectives. This can help to ensure that investment decisions are made in a strategic and thoughtful manner, rather than based on emotions or impulses.

Lastly, it is important to keep in mind that investing during a recession requires discipline and self-control. A common man should avoid getting caught up in market hype or overreacting to negative news. Instead, they should remain focused on their long-term goals and stick to their investment strategy, even during challenging times. By following these principles and making informed investment decisions, a common man can turn a recession into a profitable opportunity and build wealth over the long term.

In conclusion, making informed and strategic investments during a recession can be a valuable opportunity for a common man. By educating themselves, diversifying their portfolio, following key principles, and maintaining discipline, a common man can reduce risk and improve their chances of earning a profit in a challenging economic environment. By taking a long-term perspective and making thoughtful investment decisions, a common man can build wealth and achieve financial security for themselves and their family.

CHAPTER TWENTY-SEVEN

Being financially agile in changing times

Being financially agile in changing times, especially during a recession, is crucial for maintaining and improving one's financial well-being. A recession is a period of economic decline characterized by a decrease in GDP (Gross Domestic Product), rising unemployment, and declining consumer spending. It can have a significant impact on an individual's financial stability and long-term financial goals. However, by being financially agile, one can not only weather the storm of a recession but also use it as an opportunity to grow their wealth. In this essay, we will discuss how a common man can become financially agile during a recession.

The first step in being financially agile during a recession is to understand the basics of economics and how recessions work. It is important to have a general understanding of how economic cycles work and what factors contribute to a recession. This knowledge will help you make informed financial decisions and prepare for the inevitable ups and downs of the economy.

The next step is to identify opportunities in a downturn. Recessions can create opportunities for those who are willing to look for them. For example, the stock market tends to be more volatile during a recession, and smart investors can take advantage of this to buy undervalued stocks that have the potential to grow in value over time. Real estate prices may also decrease during a recession, providing an opportunity for savvy investors to purchase properties at a discount.

Building a recession-proof portfolio is another way to become financially agile during a recession. This means investing in a diversified mix of assets that are less likely to be affected by economic downturns. A well-balanced portfolio should include a mix of stocks, bonds, and other assets that have the potential to provide a steady stream of income even during a recession. This will help reduce the overall risk of your investments and ensure that you have a steady source of income during uncertain times.

Real estate investments during a recession can also be a wise decision for a common man. Although real estate prices may decrease during a recession, they tend to bounce back quickly once the economy starts to recover. By investing in real estate during a downturn, a common man can take advantage of lower prices and the potential for higher returns when the market improves. However, it is important to do your research and invest in properties that are likely to hold their value over the long term.

Stock market strategies during a recession can also be beneficial for a common man. While it is true that the stock market tends to be more volatile during a recession, it can also provide opportunities for growth. A common man can consider investing in blue-chip stocks that have a history of stability and growth, or in companies that are less likely to be affected by a recession. It is important to do your research and invest in well-established companies with a solid track record.

Maximizing savings and reducing expenses is another key to becoming financially agile during a recession. By reducing unnecessary expenses and increasing your savings rate, you can build a financial cushion that will help you weather the storm of a recession. This can include cutting back on luxury items, reducing your overall spending, and looking for ways to save money on daily expenses.

Navigating unemployment and job loss is also important during a recession. With unemployment rates typically rising during a recession, it is essential to have a backup plan in case you lose your job. This could include having an emergency fund to cover expenses, exploring alternative sources of income, or developing new skills that can help you find work in a different field.

Entrepreneurship is another way for a common man to become financially agile during a recession. With unemployment rates on the rise, starting a business can provide an opportunity to secure a steady source of income and take control of your financial future. This can involve starting a small business

CHAPTER TWENTY-EIGHT

Building a recession-resilient business

Building a recession-resilient business during a recession is a challenging but important task for entrepreneurs and small business owners. The 2008 global financial crisis highlighted the importance of being prepared for tough economic times, and while no one can predict the future, taking steps to ensure that your business is prepared for a downturn can go a long way in securing its long-term success.

First and foremost, it is important to understand the dynamics of a recession and how it affects businesses. A recession is a period of economic contraction characterized by a decline in gross domestic product, increased unemployment, and reduced consumer spending. During this time, businesses are faced with a number of challenges, including decreased demand for their products or services, reduced access to capital, and increased competition from struggling firms looking to stay afloat.

To build a recession-resilient business, it is crucial to focus on the fundamentals of your business model. This includes maintaining strong financial discipline, such as keeping expenses under control and avoiding excessive debt. It is also important to focus on developing a solid customer base, building a reputation for quality, and ensuring that you are providing value to your customers in the form of high-quality products or services.

Another important step in building a recession-resilient business is to diversify your revenue streams. This means looking for new business opportunities and expanding into new markets, as well as finding ways to increase the value of your existing products or services. For example, if you run a small retail business, you could consider offering online sales or creating a loyalty program to increase customer engagement.

In addition to diversifying your revenue streams, it is also important to develop strong relationships with suppliers and partners. During a recession, many businesses struggle to secure the resources they need to continue operating, but having a strong network of suppliers and partners can help you weather the storm. By developing strong relationships, you can also negotiate better deals and take advantage of opportunities that may arise during a downturn.

One of the biggest challenges that businesses face during a recession is reduced consumer spending, but there are ways to overcome this. One strategy is to focus on meeting the needs of cost-conscious consumers. This could involve offering more affordable products or services, or finding ways to increase the value of your offerings. For example, you could offer a loyalty program or bundle products and services together to create a more appealing package for customers.

Another strategy for building a recession-resilient business is to take advantage of technological advancements. The internet and social media have created new opportunities for businesses to reach customers and market their products or services. By leveraging these tools, you can reach new customers, increase your brand awareness, and improve customer engagement.

Finally, it is important to have a plan in place for managing the impact of a recession on your business. This includes having contingency plans for reducing expenses and cutting costs, as well as strategies for securing capital and finding alternative sources of funding. By having a plan in place, you can make informed decisions and take swift action to mitigate the impact of a downturn on your business.

In conclusion, building a recession-resilient business is a key challenge for entrepreneurs and small business owners, but it is possible with the right approach. By focusing on the fundamentals of your business model, diversifying your revenue streams, building strong relationships, and utilizing technology, you can ensure that your business is prepared for a downturn and ready to weather any economic storm. Additionally, having a plan in place for managing the impact of a recession can help you make informed decisions and take swift action to protect your business during tough times.

CHAPTER TWENTY-NINE

Planning for unexpected events and emergencies

Planning for Unexpected Events and Emergencies during a Recession

A recession is a period of economic decline, characterized by a decline in gross domestic product (GDP), rising unemployment, and declining economic activity. During these times, it's crucial to have a plan in place to deal with unexpected events and emergencies. These can range from job loss, unexpected medical expenses, to natural disasters. In this essay, we'll discuss how a common man can prepare for and respond to these situations during a recession.

First, it's important to understand that during a recession, emergency funds become even more crucial. An emergency fund is a set amount of money saved for unexpected expenses and emergencies. Having an emergency fund can provide a sense of financial security during a recession, as it can help cover expenses without dipping into other investments or taking on additional debt.

A good rule of thumb is to aim for three to six months' worth of living expenses in an emergency fund. This should cover expenses such as housing, food, transportation, and healthcare.

Second, it's crucial to have a budget in place. This can help identify areas where you can reduce expenses, freeing up funds to put into an emergency fund. A budget can also help prioritize spending during a recession, ensuring that essential expenses are taken care of first. Additionally, it's important to continuously monitor and adjust your budget as circumstances change.

Third, it's essential to have insurance coverage in place. Insurance can help cover expenses in case of job loss, unexpected medical expenses, or other emergencies. The types of insurance needed will depend on your individual circumstances, but commonly recommended types include health insurance, life insurance, and disability insurance. It's also important to regularly review your insurance coverage and adjust it as needed.

Fourth, it's crucial to have a plan for reducing debt during a recession. High levels of debt can become a significant burden during a recession, making it more difficult to respond to unexpected events and emergencies. To reduce debt, it's important to prioritize paying off high-interest debt, such as credit card debt, first. Additionally, it's essential to avoid taking on new debt and instead focus on reducing existing debt.

Fifth, it's important to have a plan for continuing to build wealth during a recession. This can be done by taking advantage of market dislocations and investing in stocks, real estate, or other assets that are undervalued. However, it's crucial to only make informed and strategic investments, avoiding high-risk investments that could result in significant losses. Additionally, it's essential to have a long-term financial plan that takes into account your individual circumstances and goals.

Finally, it's important to stay informed and prepared for unexpected events and emergencies during a recession. This means having a plan in place for dealing with job loss, natural disasters, or other emergencies. It also means staying informed about economic conditions and staying up-to-date with changes to government programs and assistance that can help during a recession.

In conclusion, a recession can be a challenging time for a common man, but with the right planning and preparation, it's possible to respond to unexpected events and emergencies. This includes having an emergency fund, a budget, insurance coverage, a plan for reducing debt, and a plan for building wealth. Additionally, it's crucial to stay informed and prepared for unexpected events and emergencies, having a plan in place to deal with these situations as they arise. With these steps in place, a common man can weather a recession and come out on the other side in a better financial position.

CHAPTER THIRTY

Embracing change and embracing opportunity

Embracing change and embracing opportunity are two key elements to thriving during a recession. A recession can be a difficult time for many people, but it can also offer a unique set of opportunities for those who are prepared to seize them. In this essay, we will explore the benefits of embracing change and opportunity during a recession and offer practical advice for those looking to make the most of this difficult time.

Recessions can be challenging, but they can also present unique opportunities for growth and development. When the economy slows down, many people are faced with job loss, reduced income, and increased financial stress. However, with the right approach, these challenges can be turned into opportunities for growth and progress. For example, recessions can provide a chance to re-evaluate your financial priorities and make changes that will better position you for long-term success.

One of the key benefits of embracing change during a recession is that it can help you to stay flexible and adaptable in the face of uncertainty. As the economy changes, it can be easy to get stuck in old habits and patterns, but by embracing change, you can be better equipped to navigate the challenges that come your way. This can involve taking steps to improve your financial situation, such as reducing expenses, increasing your income, or developing new sources of income.

Another benefit of embracing change during a recession is that it can help you to develop new skills and knowledge. For example, if you lose your job during a recession, this can be an opportunity to learn a new trade or develop a new skill that will help you to better succeed in the future. Additionally, during a recession, there are often a wealth of free resources available to help people develop their skills and knowledge, such as online courses, workshops, and mentorship programs.

Embracing opportunity during a recession is also critical to success. When the economy slows down, many businesses and individuals become more risk-averse, which can limit the number of opportunities available. However, by embracing opportunity, you can be better positioned to seize new opportunities as they arise. This may involve taking calculated risks, such as starting a business or investing in a new venture.

To embrace opportunity during a recession, it is important to stay informed and educated about economic trends and changes. This can involve reading financial news and analysis, attending workshops and conferences, or working with a financial advisor. Additionally, by building strong relationships and networks, you can increase your chances of learning about new opportunities and being in a position to take advantage of them.

In addition to embracing change and opportunity, it is also important to have a strong financial foundation during a recession. This can involve reducing expenses, increasing your savings, and developing a solid financial plan. By taking these steps, you can better position yourself to weather the economic storms of a recession and be better equipped to take advantage of new opportunities that may arise.

In conclusion, embracing change and embracing opportunity are two key elements to thriving during a recession. While a recession can be a difficult time, it can also offer a unique set of opportunities for those who are prepared to seize them. By staying flexible and adaptable, developing new skills and knowledge, embracing opportunity, and having a strong financial foundation, you can better position yourself for success during a recession and beyond.

Printed by Libri Plureos GmbH in Hamburg, Germany